Computer Use Induced Stresses

What you need to Know

By

Adetutu Ijose

Published By:

Jointheirs Publishing

JP

Computer Use Induced Stress:
What you need to Know

Jointheirs Publishing
Jointheirs Activities Incorporated
www.jointheirspublishing.com

ISBN – 1-46354-345-X

EAN – 978-1-46354-345-7

Printed in the United States of America

COMPUTER USE INDUCED STRESS:

WHAT YOU NEED TO KNOW

An Important Caution

The advice given in *Computer Use Induced Stress* is based on an understanding of the effects of computer use on human health gained when I suffered life threatening consequences of computer use and began to understand the human code of existence from studying the human machine user manual we call the Bible or Scriptures.

Many people may not attribute the feelings of being overwhelmed, unappreciated, not getting enough cooperation from colleagues or understood that they feel to their computer use.

Computer use is actually very stressful to the body and it is not a stress our bodies are coded to handle for computer use violates many of our natural coded way of existence as humans.

This book is informational and is a guide that contains both advice and instructions. It is essential that you read the entire book carefully and that any decision you make be discussed with your physician before proceeding.

This book is intended to be a health and lifestyle help.

What it will do is provide information to enable the reader understand the biological issues behind the daily burnout they experience from computer use.

It will assist in taking decisions about gaining a better understanding of what responsible computer use entails.

It is important to remember that any guidelines established must be followed through to be successful. It is my hope that as people read this book they will better understand the limitations that have been put in place by our maker in nature to prevent us from hurting ourselves and learn to operate within those boundaries to avoid self-destructive actions.

For more detailed reading about the health effects of computer use and how to minimize them, please get hold of my books *Lessons I Learned the Hard Way, Computer Use addiction and withdrawal syndrome* and all my other books in print and in ebook version available at amazon.com and other online store.

A complete listing of my available books at the time of writing is provided at the end of this book under the section titled "Note to the Reader". You may also want to visit my website www.foodsthathealdaily.com

The understanding gained from this book will assist individuals in identifying the various health-related changes that are going on in their lives as a result of the effect of computer-related activities on the brain, nerves, muscles, and various organs of their bodies.

These effects are the consequence of the unnatural nature of the computer-use environment on our bodies. For example, we do not look directly at the sun our natural coded light for reading to read but we look directly at the computer light to read creating unnatural stresses in our body's system it was not designed for.

This book could also assist in communicating during discussions with physicians to avoid being misdiagnosed as psychotic for example

In summary in this book, I am trying to shed light on some of the health problems that are inherent in computer use when proper preventative measures are not put in place to protect the human machine.

This is only a guide, and individual situations will definitely vary.

If you are under treatment for any computer-related behavioral disorder or if you suspect you might need such care, you must discuss any insight you gain from this book with your doctor before starting.

Table of Contents

Chapter 1
Biochemicals and Stress

The health effects of stress are manifested in many ways by the human body. Sometimes it shows up as things like cancer, digestive problems cold, lung issues, heart problems and so on.

Sometimes stress manifests as behavioral and mental stress the most commonly known of which is depression.

According to Medline plus [1-1] Depression is a serious medical illness that involves the brain. It's more than just a feeling of being "down in the dumps" or "blue" for a few days.

According to the article, the feelings do not go away. They persist and interfere with your everyday life. It provided the following as some of the symptoms of depression:

1. Sadness

2. Loss of interest or pleasure in activities you used to enjoy

3. Change in weight

4. Difficulty sleeping or oversleeping

5. Energy loss

6. Feelings of worthlessness

7. Thoughts of death or suicide

Depression is a disorder of the brain. There are a variety of causes, including genetic, environmental, psychological, and biochemical factors

Chapter 2
Depression Statistics

The NIMH [2-1] states that Major depressive disorder is one of the most common mental disorders in the United States.

This assessment was based on Statistic from Substance Abuse and Mental Health Services Administration (SAMHSA).

There was some good news in the statistics. Though depression is very common, statistics seemed to indicate s that 12 months prevalence of depression among adults aged 18 – 25 grew from was down from 9.7 to 8.7% from year 2005 to 2008.

Between ages 26 – 29 it declined from 8.4 to 7.5% and for 50+ it declined from 5.1 to 4.5%

This seemingly good trend may actually mean that more people are self-medicating or trying to use homeopathic, herbs, diet and exercise to solve their problems rather than seeking medical help in a bid to avoid medication.

With the ever-increasing number of cases people see at work and in society, the seeming good news may not be telling the story but that is what we have.

There is no way to officially know that someone is depressed unless that seek medical attention that is recorded.

Demographically, the SAMHSA statistics reveal some interesting facts including the following:

1. Statistics by Sex: Women are 70% more likely to experience depression during their lifetime

2. Statistics by Race: Non Hispanic whites are 40% more likely to experience depression during their lifetime

3. Compared to adults over the age of 60 years, 18 – 29 year olds are 70% more likely to have experienced depression over their lifetime, 30 –44year olds are 120% more likely and 45 to 59 year olds are 100% more likely.

An April 2011 SAMSHA News Release 2-2 said the following:

"A new national report released in conjunction with Mental Health Awareness Month and Children's Mental Health Awareness Day indicates that 8.1 percent of America's adolescents aged 12 to 17 (2 million youth) experienced at least one major depressive episode (MDE) in the past year.

The report by the Substance Abuse and Mental Health Services Administration (SAMHSA) also shows that only 34.7 percent of these adolescents suffering from major depressive episodes received treatment during this period."

It further said that "Depression among adolescents is a serious public health problem that is all too often overlooked and the consequences can be devastating," said SAMHSA Administrator, Pamela S. Hyde, J.D. "If depression among young people is identified and treated early we can turn a life around and reduce the impact of mental illness and substance abuse on America's communities."

One of the study's most notable findings was that adolescents who had suffered from a Mental Depressive Episode (MDE) in the past year were more than three times as likely as those without a past year MDE to have had a substance use disorder in the past year (18.9 percent versus 6 percent).

The study also found significant differences in the rates of past year MDE experiences among subgroups of adolescents.

For example, adolescent females were twice as likely as their male counterparts to have experienced a past year MDE (11.7 percent versus 4.7 percent). Rates of past year MDE experience also rose as adolescents grew older with rates increasing from 3.6 percent of adolescents aged 12 to 10.4 percent of adolescents aged 15.

This statistical information is all well and good. There is however something missing that no one seems willing to acknowledge – the fact that computer use may be a factor in depression.

While the link to substance abuse is being investigated, the link to computer use exposure is conveniently ignored.

Here may be the reason, Computers have become indispensable to our modern way of doing business and living and some people may erroneously be concerned that focusing on its effect could affect the economy.

Contrary to this, it is the opposite that is true. It is not acknowledging the problem and the resultant destruction of too many lives that will force many people to abandon computer use whether they like it or not and when such people become large enough in number, the national and indeed global economy we are all trying so hard to protect may fall on its head with no means of saving it.

For example, though many people are aware of the compulsive computer use by teenagers, many are unaware of its health consequences though they would admit that teenagers are addicted to computers and computer devices such as cell phones, ipods, video games and so on. It seems the tendency is to explain things away with anything else.

The truth is that computer use need not be so devastating on health. True computers will always hurt however our loving maker knowing we would come to such a time as this has already provided many things in nature to ensure we do not self destroy.

What we need to do is exercise some humility admit we are living computers created by a loving creator and learn from the user manual he has given us what we need to do and be careful to acknowledge we got the information from him so it can be a blessing to us as a generation on earth.

Indeed long term computer use can either be a blessing or a curse. We all get to choose which it will be.

In this book I will be sharing many of these natural preventive and management methods I learned the hard way because there was no one to tell me. In fact no one even acknowledge that computer use could hurt.

Chapter 3
Teenage Depression and computer Use

The high level of stress inherent in computer use and the resultant nutrient, nerve and brain messaging biochemical depletions may be creating depression like symptoms in today's teenagers

According to a September 27, 2010 [4-1] article of the National Institute for Mental Health (NIMH), National Survey Confirms that Youth are Disproportionately Affected by Mental Disorders.

This observation was based on NIMH survey published in the October 2010 issue of the *Journal of the American Academy of Child and Adolescent Psychiatry* that said that about 20 percent of U.S. youth during their lifetime are affected by some type of mental disorder to an extent that they have difficulty functioning,

The article said that this finding supports the observation from surveys of adults that mental disorders most commonly start in early life.

There are many kinds of mental issues. Wikipedia the online dictionary defines mental disorders as " a psychological or behavioral pattern generally associated with subjective distress or disability that occurs in an individual, and which is not a part of normal development or culture. Such a disorder may consist of a combination of affective, behavioural, cognitive and perceptual components'.

They actually reveal the individual's inability to cope with some certain stresses that overtask and consequently overwhelm the inbuilt coping mechanisms.

This essentially means a depletion in inhibitory neurotransmitters responsible for handling stresses placed upon his or her behavioral coping mechanism beyond which the body is able to quickly rebound from.

These disorders include depression, manic behavior, anxiety and so on.

Depression is a mental issue that can be caused by a host of issues including, genetics, stress, chemical imbalance and so on, according to the national women's health information center [4-2]

At least two of these factors stress and chemical imbalance are inherent in computer use, making users susceptible to various mental issues including depression and or depression like symptoms. These imbalances and stresses could also make those with genetical susceptibility more at risk.

The risk for teenagers is increased by the fact that their brains and body functions are still in the developing phase. This constant rapid brain change can also mask the problem for a long time before it is detected.

The fact is that the use of computer devices of all kinds including iphones, cell phones, video games, classroom teaching and learning devises in school and at home for study and recreation may be placing unusually high demand on the body's nutrient, nerve and brain messaging biochemicals beyond what the growing body can effectively handle. This has serious implications as well as future implications for today's youths.

The lure of light generating devises may be too much for teenagers to handle without parental control. If parents are not vigilant the trouble may not be detected for a long time.

Today's modern living environment places teenagers in the presence of artificial light for most of the 24 hours of the day as children read and work in school rooms and homes that do not allow in enough natural reading light during the day.

To make things worse for the body, children no longer get sent to bed early. We stretch the daytime artificially at night with artificial lights placing the human natural coded time clock under enormous stress, working when our bodies are coded to be at rest, growing and self-repairing.

When we add incessant bombardment from computer devices, we place the growing body's coping system at risk.

If parents do not notice the problem until behavioral issues become out of hand, there could be permanent damage done that would have implication for the rest of a child's life.

Indeed the modern times places enormous pressure on parents with regards to parenting and being the guardians of their children.

Hence due to technology parenting has become much more difficult than in previous generation. On the other the need to work long hours in order to put food on the table for these same children is more acute than for previous generations.

Thus while the child needs the parent's attention, the parent needs to spend more time trying to provide for the child. This conflict in many cases results in children being allowed to be on computer devices for too long.

It may therefore be a good preventive measure for parents and schools to monitor and set limits for computer use and exposure for these children. They may complain as teenager will always do and feel stifled but the discipline and the health issues they avoid is worth the trouble.

It may indeed also be a good thing for parents to spend quality time talking to their children to find out how computer use and internet exposure especially social websites, games, the news they read and online comments are affecting them. This should be done regularly

Further if any stressful incidence occurs locally or internationally that children get to know about, it is advisable to talk it out with them instead of allowing them to use their computers as their comforter as many people both children and adults seem to be doing in today's world.

A computer is lifeless and cannot convey or filter emotions and can therefore not be a source of comfort for emotional stress. Reliance on it could therefore lead to feelings of emptiness, loneliness, anger, and depression and so on as serious biochemical imbalances set in.

Going for daily walks in the daytime and absorbing sunlight which is life containing and which is naturally coded to stimulate our brains to produce emotion balancing biochemicals as well as exercising, prayer, forgiving, talking to others, reading (especially reading the human computer user manual we call the Bible to gain a better understanding of how we are coded to be) and eating foods that provide the nutrients needed by the brain to produce these biochemicals would be a better bet.

If you want to know more about how computer use affects behavior and why this is so get my various books available in both print and ebook versions at amazon.com and other online stores. A complete listing of my available books at the time of writing this book is provided in this book in the section titled "Note to the Reader.

The technology age is indeed a difficult one for parents. Computers, the Internet, video games, cell phones and so one are all double-edged tools. They are useful for quick communication and carrying our some certain tasks as well as for keeping the children busy.

The problem is that their use must be monitored and controlled to prevent them from becoming a curse. Secondly, once in place, parents need to enforce the controls they put in place.

Children cannot be left to control themselves. That part of the brain is not yet full developed in them. Even if they seem responsible parents need to follow up to avoid irreparable surprises.

Chapter 4
Adult Computer Use Induced Stress

Computer use, because it is unnatural to our normal coded way of existence, is inherently stressful to our body's system, which has to try to accommodate a process it is not coded with.

It is like trying to get a word processing program to do some calculation like a spreadsheet. At the end of the day the only way to do it is to externally do the calculation and add the figure to the table.

Trying to make the word processing software handle calculation will not work as the process code is not in it and consequently cannot be performed.

In the case of the computer, we humans are able to use it, but it with a lot of strain on the body's stress management system. The body is a living computer coded with some flexibility. It has a lot of constraint and boundaries in it that manifest in the action of motion such as walking talking eating.

These actions are based upon myriads of constraints and boundaries placed on excitative neurotransmitters responsible for motion to ensure we have controlled motion such as the controlled motion we call walking for example.

Without these constraints we would not be able to exist as humans on earth. Since the foundation of our being hinges on discipline, small wonder uncontrolled activities and actions whatever they may be are problematic to us as humans.

The unnatural stress we expose ourselves to as during computer use could, over time, result in life threatening health issues. The body's stress management system will become overburdened and begin to breakdown if we do not make some lifestyle changes to make the process less stressful to our bodies.

Consequently, the good news is that, though the computer will always hurt, the hurt can be minimized to a point where it is not devastating and does not have the potential of ruining our lives and careers.

One thing to bear in mind if, at the moment, you feel you do not need help is that computer use stress develops over time. Mine took over 20 years of being ignored to finally result in life threatening issues the medical profession could neither diagnose nor treat. I learned the hard way so that you would not have to.

Please learn from my experience. I am a living miracle. I would like to help you avoid my pitfall because you may not be able to climb out successfully. It took divine intervention in my case. That does not happen everyday. We are all supposed to learn from each other's experience.

I am going to make this chapter very easy to understand.

There are many levels of stress we encounter in computer use. In this book I will focus on 10 (ten) easy to understand issues to give us an idea of what the issues are.

1. We do not look directly at the sun - the source of light we are coded with and which we read with naturally.

2. The computer light is at close range contrary to the huge distance between the sun and us, which makes

sunlight highly diffused and easier to bear by the time it reaches our eyes and skin.

3. Computer light is not natural. It is artificially generated and so not fully compatible with our system. It is in fact toxic to our souls. The only light compatible with us is that from the sun, moon and stars. These are the only ones we are coded with.

   Our bodies can handle them without stress as a built in stress management system has been coded into us to manage it. For example, research shows that we blink 66% less on the computer. This is very stressful for the brain, which uses the blink function to take constant rest from the sunlight when we are outside and in direct contact with sunlight.

4. A fourth issue is the fact that computer use involves the exercising of only a few muscles. This is contrary to our natural coded way of exercising most of our body's muscles in concert when performing life's functions. It creates a lot of stress in our musculoskeletal system.

5. The computer exposes us to various toxic chemicals emitting off the computer monitor screen and from laptop and desktop CPU backs and sides as well as laptop cords and batteries.

6. The act of being in the presence of light is an activity that consumes a lot of vitamins and minerals such as iron, vitamin D, B, C, Zinc, Magnesium and so on. We however do not normally structure our diets and meals with the nutritional requirement for computer use in mind

7. Printed words that our bodies are coded for are static on paper. Pixels i.e. words on computer screens are not static forcing our eye muscle to continually focus and refocus resulting in the weakening of the eye muscles.

8. Operating computers produce a lot of positive ions resulting in an ionization imbalance in the environments they operate. This is what is responsible for the headaches, sneezing and allergy like symptoms we feel when as computer users.

9. Computer light every other light dehydrates the environment in which it is present. This is what results in the dry eyes. It is the drying of the skin around the eyes. That is why eye drops do not resolve computer use related dry eyes.

10. Everything is nature is a coding together of various electromagnetic field to produce objects that emit light continuously to manifest them in a way that they can be seen.

    Hence exposure to artificial electromagnetic field not coded for humans to be exposed to results in compromises to our system right down to the cell level. Over time this could result in major system breakdowns we call sickness and diseases

It is obvious from the above that computer use subjects our system to enormous physiological stress. These stresses manifest in the form of headaches, insomnia, asthma, allergy like symptoms, dry eyes and so on.

There are also behavioral issues such as, feeling of being overwhelmed, risky behavior, inability to understand or keep boundaries, lack of self control, feeling of imbalance and life getting out of hand, inability to focus on a task, physical and mental exhaustion and so on.

Vision problems result from stress to the eye muscles, which as we have read in this chapter has to continually focus and refocus constantly in a bid to read pixels off the computer screen. Printed words in contrast are static and do not need constant focusing and refocusing.

There are also musculoskeletal issues that resemble carpel tunnel syndrome, tendonitis and other musculoskeletal issues.

In the case of computer related stress, they arise from nerve eye issues that radiate through the neck, shoulders and arms and right down to the finger and resemble carpel tunnel syndrome. Tendonitis mimicking pain goes right down to the soles of the feet.

In addition to all this there are also brain stress related issues arising from the fact that lifeless light cannot stimulate the brain to produce neurotransmitters, like gamma-amino butyric acid (GABA) and other inhibitory neurotransmitters that help our brains and body system handle stress. These biochemicals need life containing light to stimulate the brain to activate their production. Consequently we feel relaxed in sunlight but anxious and stressed in the presence of computer light.

The depletion of GABA and other biochemicals and minerals required for brain messaging functions is what is responsible for the feeling of being overwhelmed we feel on the job and other anxiety issues. These could be as serious as panic attacks, life threatening levels of insomnia and chest pains, comprehension, memory and speech related issues and so on.

These stresses could result in just about any kind of issue including cancer, liver cysts, gallstones, feeling of breathlessness, feeling faint and excessive fatigue.

Excessive cortisol is secreted, which can also lead to weight gain and other related issues.

The difference between computer use induced stress related issues and those arising from other stresses is the fact that they do not resolve with medication.

That is because the issues arise as a result o the absence of life containing light needed for stress management functions. Hence, the problem is not at the physical level but at the soul level, where the light is processed, and that controls the physical parts that we can touch.

Computer use related stresses are however not well understood by the medical profession and are consequently routinely misdiagnosed for other more commonly understood forms of stress.

 The medical profession cannot, however, be blamed. It is not taught in medical school. We are a society that believes that everything should and must be resolved by medication. Hence, doctors are required to prescribe medication to avoid litigation.

All is however not lost. As we read in the preceding chapter, many people erroneously believe that if the issue of computer related health conditions are known and acknowledged, the economy would be affected as people choose not to use the computer.

Remember that as we have read, nothing can be further from the truth.

It is the lack of acknowledgment and knowing about this issue that is a silent, ignored global epidemic that is threatening to overburden our finances with health care costs, an ever revolving cycle of medication, when we try to medicate an issue that cannot be resolved by medication as the sufferer's condition worsens.

It is not handling the issue the right way that will make people become incapacitated and unable to continue using the computer regardless of whether they want to use it or not.

Women Specific issues;

In chapter 2 we read that women are disproportionately affected by depression more than men.

Computer usage is stressful to our brains and consumes a lot of its resources. This can leave women more prone to mental issues such as anxiety and depression

As an Information Technology professional with over 20 years intensive computer use experience who has experienced first hand the many horrible effects of computer use on my health. Some were even life threatening, I want to share some of the things I now know about the effects of computer use on women's mental health and how to minimize them.

Computers as we have read in this book are here to stay and indeed have become indispensable to our modern way of living.

The computer use environment is however unnatural to our natural way of not looking directly at a source of light and is consequently excessively stressful and toxic to our brains and other body organs.

As women therefore, we need to have a lifestyle that reduces the stress from other sources if we want to be avid users of computers without hurting ourselves.

Simple changes such as eating organic foods especially, fruits, vegetables and whole grain meals can go a long way in helping us achieve these goals. Herbicides, pesticides and man made fertilizers infuse many chemicals into the foods they are applied to that are not normally occurring in those foods.

These chemicals make these foods more difficult for our digestive systems to handle resulting in the excessive utilization of the body's stress and immune system resources in digestion leaving a much smaller amount for other body processes.

When this happens our brains do not have enough resources to handle other stresses resulting in feelings of anxiety, depression, unhappiness and other relational and behavioral problems etc.

Thus we can see that eating foods that require the use fewer resources for digestion will make it easier for our brains to handle the excessive stress arising from the unnatural nature of computer use.

Another simple thing that can be done is exercising both indoors and outdoors most especially walking as this exercises all our muscles while getting all the benefits of the sun and exposure to fresh air. This is natural to our way of existence and very relaxing to the brain and all our other body organs.

There are many other computer related health issues. For example, when we see with our eyes, it is actually our brain that does the seeing. Our eyes are like the camera that the brain uses to see hence the pollution laden light rays from the computer could create harmful effects on our brain.

Eating brain health foods and exercising are important simple steps that could help reduce computer related depression, psychotic behavior etc. arising from excessive stress to our brains from computer use.

These tips are some of the ways in which as women we can help ourselves

Chapter 5
Stress Management Suggestions

Whatever you do must be discussed with your doctor. Just look for one who is ready to go beyond medication. Send your doctor this book and my other books and discuss your issues with him or her..

Please refer to Note to the Reader for a complete listing of my books and information on how to obtain your copies.

The various solutions that help in managing and minimizing this problem are very simple, are mostly not expensive and are not onerous. The only thing is that they must be done and done consistently. There is a long list.

However for the purpose of this book I will give a few tips.

1. Crack open the window and allow the fresh air in. If you can, work beside a window and crack it open even in winter. Just put on the heater and adjust the thermostat up.

    You need the air around you to automatically rebalance itself constantly as it does outside.

2. You need to avoid excessive toxins. Therefore, eat organic to avoid additional toxins from pesticides and other artificial chemicals and pesticides to avoid overwhelming the system.

3. Eat a lot of fruits and vegetables and whole grains to provide the nutrients that are heavily depleted by computer use and whose depletions are indicated in most common stresses (e.g. magnesium, iron, vitamin, D, C, B and so on).

4. Be outdoors as much as possible. Go for daily walks and let your eyes rest on the green grass and feast on the outdoor beauty they were designed to look at. If you can, do some outdoor sports.

5. Drink water instead of soda.

6. Pray. I will not be politically correct here. My advice is pray in the name of Jesus. This is the way the human computer user manual we call the Bible tells us to pray.

7. Drink freshly made juices instead of packaged juices

8. Avoid processed food

9. Do a cleanse e.g. using a juicing method. Do this under the monitoring eyes of your doctor

10. Take many breaks from the computer. Try to look away every 30 minutes. Take mini, micro and long beaks. Talk to others.

11. Establish good healthy familial relationships so as not to lose touch with your humanness and to avoid virtual entrapment. Do not isolate yourself.

12. Take each day at a time. Tomorrow will take care of itself.

13. Avoid anger. Take a deep breath. Things may not be as bad as they seem.

14. Read with the light of the sun daily. The best thing to read is the Bible, for the essence is to fill your soul with

abundance of life containing light so that your limited exposure to lifeless light does not overwhelm the soul.

15. It is the overwhelming of the soul that we feel as stress. If possible, get the Bible on CD as well so that you can also listen to it as background sound when working. This especially works if you work from home and are more in control of your environment.

16. Listen to gospel music that tells you about God's love

17. Make ergonomic changes to your workstation. Ensure proper computer desk height and proper hand rest height, etc

18. Let the sunlight in when using the computer so your brain can be stimulated to produce light stress managing neurotransmitters such as GABA, Serotonin and so on thereby reducing the effect of their depetion as a result of computer use.

19. Try some inconspicuous body stretches at your desk. Make sure you do not draw attention to avoid getting in trouble.

20. Join a gym if you can afford it. However, note that going to the gym is no replacement for outdoor exercise. Do both indoor and outdoor exercises every day.

Everything you do must be in consultation of your doctor. Computer related stress should never be handled as a self-help issue. If you are already suffering, you may need blood work and monitoring done.

For more detailed and comprehensive information, please get hold of my various books. They are available at amazon.com in print and kindle version for you and your doctor. Read them all and decide on a plan of action together with your doctor. Also visit my websites www.computeragehealthrisk.com and www.foodsthathealdaily.com. Here, you can get hold of my various articles.

I hope I have begun to open your eyes to the need for action. Ignorance is not an option for anyone who wants to remain a healthy long-term computer user.

Note to Doctors - Supplementation

It is very important to work with medical professionals.

Because of the various depletion of nutrients that occur in computer use addiction, it is important to get complete whole body chemistry analyzing the blood, urine and stool at the minimum to determine as much as possible what has been depleted in order to determine the best nutritional diet to embark upon and to determine if supplementation is necessary.

This analysis does not reveal everything but it is a very important starting point. It should be repeated as needed to track progress and determine necessary changes required in the treatment program.

In addition there will more often than not be a need for GABA and melatonin supplementation. Another thing I will recommend a doctor using is Rhodolia Rosea.

There are other issues such as magnesium, zinc, iron, Vitamin D, B, C and other mineral and vitamin supplementation, but in order to ensure people go to their doctors, I will only go this far. I invite doctors to get in touch with me via the email address provided in "Note to the reader" for more information on supplementation. You can also read my book *Lessons I Learned the Hard way.*

Computer use induced health conditions should never be self diagnosed and treated without medical help to monitor the process. It is very dangerous to try to do it on your own. Get your doctor my books and get him or her to contact me for things like checklists, supplementation and other matters I consider too risky to provide to the general public.

Note To The Reader:

About the author:

Adetutu Ijose, is a technology and accounting professional with over 25 years of intensive computer use exposure who suffered life threatening computer related health conditions the doctors could neither diagnose not treat.

In desperation and with a good knowledge of codes and how they work she studied the human computer user manual we call the Bible until she was able to understand why and how the computer hurts our body's system as well as the preventative and repair kits placed in nature by our maker.

She also began to realize that the many signs of depression and various behavioral issues many avid computer users were having was as a result of the stress of computer use.

She was able to provide advise to friends on how to assist their doctors in avoiding a misdiagnosis as well as providing advise on care for them to share with their doctors.

With the increasing report of suicide and depression among computer users, she realized that it was important to make the information she had public in a bid to help everyone.

She is now passing on her understanding about computer use induced issues through her many books, other writings and speaking activities including information about the issue of computer use induced stress to everyone so others can receive help and avoid preventable devastating consequences of computer use.

Adetutu Ijose is a speaker on the subject of computer use induced health conditions. She is also a contributor to several online article websites and blogs including content sites associatedcontent.com and examiner.com. She has also been interviewed on radio.

To schedule a speaking or consulting engagement, interview, so on with the author, please contact Adetutu Ijose at http://www.foodsthathealdaily.com.

For Adetutu Ijose's online press kit or for press releases and other media matters and inquiries, please go to http://lessosilearnedthehardway.com/AdetutuIjoseMediaPre ssKit.aspx

Discover other titles by Adetutu Ijose to help you better understand responsible computer use and how computer use affect us all as well as what we need to do to prevent and manage these issues at www.foodsthathealydaily.com, www.amazon.com and other online stores. Ebook versions of this and other books by Adetutu Ijose are available at amazon.com, Barnes and Nobles, Smashword.com and other ebook stores. A complete list is provided below.

Connect with Adetutu Ijose Online:
Facebook: http://www.facebook.com/home.php

Computer Use Induced Health Conditions related books by Adetutu Ijose as at the time of writing are:

1) *Lessons I Learned the Hard Way: How to Identify, Minimize, Treat and Manage Computer Related Health Condition*

2) *Computer Related Health Condition: Understanding the Human Computer*

3) *Healing Juicing Smoothie and Milk Shake Recipes: Juices, Smoothies and Milk Shakes that Help the Body Achieve its Self Healing Process*

4) *Healing Meals Recipe: Meals that Help the Body Achieve its Self Healing Process*

5) *Cyber Bullying: How and Why Bullies operate*

6) *Global Epidemic: The Human Abuse of the Computer*

7) *Computer Use Addiction and Withdrawal Syndromes: What You Need to Know*

8) *Teenage and Adult Texting Addictions: What You Need to Know*

9) *Allergies, Asthma and Computer Use: The Contributory Effects of Computer Use to Allergies and Asthma Trends*

10) *Computer Use Induced Stress: What You Need to Know*

For other titles published after this book – *Computer Use Induced Stress* please go to amazon.com and other online stores or visit my website www.foodsthathealdaily.com

References

1-1   Medline Plus A service of the U.S. National Library
         of Medicine
         National Institutes of Health
         http://www.nlm.nih.gov/medlineplus/depression.html

2-1 National Institute of Mental Health (NIMH) article on
         Major Depressive Disorder among Adults
         http://www.nimh.nih.gov/statistics/1MDD_ADULT.s
         html

2-2 April 20011 SAMHSA News Release
         http://www.samhsa.gov/newsroom/advisories/110428
         1931.aspx

4-1 NIMH article on national survey confirming rise in
         teenage mental health issues
         http://www.nimh.nih.gov/science-
         news/2010/national-survey-confirms-that-youth-are-
         disproportionately-affected-by-mental-disorders.shtml

4-2 Wikipedia the online dictionary
         http://en.wikipedia.org/wiki/Mental_disorder

4-3 The National Women's Health information Center
         womenshealth.gov webpage on Depression
         http://www.womenshealth.gov/mental-
         health/conditions/depression.cfm

INDEX

A

Abuse, 11.12, 13, 26
Addicted, 14
Addiction, 6, 33, 36
Adolescents, 12, 13
Adult, 8, 24, 43
Adults, 11, 12, 15, 18, 37
Allergy, 23
Anxiety, 16, 24, 26, 27
Artificial, 17, 22, 23, 29
Asthma, 23, 36
Author, 34, 35

B

Behavior, 7, 16, 19, 23, 28
Behavioral, 7, 9, 15, 16, 17, 23, 27, 34
Bible, 5, 19, 30, 31, 34
Biochemical, 10, 15, 18
Biochemicals, 9, 16, 18, 19, 24
Blood, 31, 33
Bodies, 5, 6, 17, 21, 22, 23
Body, 5, 6, 9, 16, 17, 20, 21, 22,24, 27, 28, 31, 33, 34, 36
Book, 5, 6, 7, 14, 21, 26, 29, 33, 36
Books, 6, 19, 29, 32, 33, 34, 35
Boundaries, 6, 20, 23
Brain, 6, 9, 10, 15, 16, 19, 22, 24, 28, 31
Brains, 16, 18, 24, 26, 29
Breaks, 30
Bullying, 36
Business, 13

C

D

E

Ebook, 6, 19, 35
Economy, 13, 14, 25
Electromagnetic, 23
Emotion, 18
Emotional, 18
Emotions, 18
Environment, 17, 23, 27, 31
Environmental, 10
Environments, 23
Ergonomic, 37
Exercise, 11, 14, 31
Exercising, 22, 27, 33, 34
Experience, 5, 12, 13, 21, 26
Eyes, 22, 23, 28, 30, 32

F

Fatigue, 25
Feelings, 5, 9, 18, 28
Fertilizers, 27
Food, 17, 30
Foods, 19, 27, 28
Fruits, 27, 29

G

GABA, 23, 31, 33
Games, 14, 16, 18, 19
Genetic, 10
Genetical, 16
Global, 14, 26, 36
Guide, 5, 7
Gym, 31

H

Headaches, 23

M

Machine, 5, 7
Magnesium, 22, 29, 33
Maker, 6, 14, 34
Medical, 11, 25, 26, 29
Medication, 11, 30, 31, 35
Memory, 24
Mental Depressive Episode, 13
Mental disorders, 11, 15
Mental exhaustion, 24
Mental Health, 11, 12, 15, 26, 37
Mental stress, 9
Messaging, 17, 19, 30
Minerals, 22, 24, 33
Motion, 20
Muscles, 6, 22, 23, 24, 27
Musculoskeletal, 22, 24

N

Nature, 6, 7
Nerve, 15, 16
Nerves, 6
Neurotransmitters, 16, 20, 24, 31
NIMH, 11, 15, 37
Nutrient, 15, 16

O

Online, 6, 15, 18, 19, 35, 36, 37
Organic, 27, 29
Organs, 6
Outdoors, 27, 30
Oversleeping, 9

P

Parenting, 17